The armed forces of the People's Republic of China (PRC) are once again on the march. Not into Vietnam or Korea or India or even Tibet, but rather in a somber, methodical march to convert their large, but outdated military, good for little more than internal security, border defense, and limited trans-border excursions, into a "leaner, meaner" fighting machine; one that will eventually transform China from a major regional power into a regional superpower possessing a credible power projection capability. This "new" China will demand not only the attention of those nations bordering it (currently 14), but the rest of Asia as well. As this modernization matures, Cambodia, Malaysia, the Philippines, South Korea, Indonesia, Japan, and even Australia will come to view the PRC in a different light.

Until recently, the PRC's armed forces resembled a 1990s version of the US Civilian Conservation Corps of the 1930s. The People's Liberation Army (PLA), and to a lesser extent the PLA Air Force (PLAAF) and PLA Navy (PLAN) were used as much to improve the agricultural and industrial productivity of the country as they were to provide a warfighting capability. However, they are now evolving into a force quite unlike that seen during the first 40 years of the PRC's existence.

The traditional strength of the PRC's military was its large land force; in sophisticated military hardware it lagged far behind many nations

1

with comparable Gross National Products (GNP). This was due in part to an over-reliance on the former Soviet Union for arms and security assistance in the 1950s and early 1960s. When a philosophical rift developed between the PRC and the USSR, and Soviet support ended, China found itself ill-prepared to assume research and development (R&D) responsibilities for much of its military.[1]

Similarly, until the mid-1960s, the defense industrial system operated under a concept that required the military to fight "an early war, an all-out war and a nuclear war." In a society that was largely agrarian, this broad tasking stretched the PRC's financial capabilities. A closed, internally-oriented defense industry evolved under highly centralized control and by design was separated from civilian industry. The defense industry also was subdivided into relatively autonomous regions and departments; little cross-communication occurred and cost effectiveness was not a concern. Also, shortly after the Chinese and the Soviets split, and the US became involved in Vietnam, China opted to build a parallel defense industry in its less vulnerable, but remote interior. Designed to be totally independent of the industrialized coastal areas, it would produce arms well after any abandonment of the traditional, more productive areas. Called the "third line" or "third front" it consisted of 2,000 facilities employing 1.35 million workers, and cost $4 billion, a considerable investment for capital-poor China in the late 1960s and early 1970s.[2]

However, the effort's productive output proved to be minimal, the program was labeled a failure, and in retrospect, it hurt the economy on a scale comparable to the economically disastrous Cultural Revolution. The program was quietly ended in the mid-1970s, and was not discussed publicly in China until 1978.[3]

This overreliance on the Soviets in the early years, combined with an inefficient, centrally controlled defense industrial infrastructure and a fear of foreign invasion all hindered China's ability to move from a relatively low technology military force to a more modern one.

DENG XIAOPING'S MODERNIZATIONS

China began to correct these mistakes when Mao Zedong died in 1976 and Deng Xiaoping eventually emerged as China's new leader. As his power base solidified, in 1978 Deng began to promote his 1973 concept of "four modernizations:" agriculture, industry, national defense, and science and technology.[4] China's military leadership responded by gradually shifting away from the Maoist "People's War" strategy of overcoming its enemies with a huge, low technology army and toward a smaller, but considerably more sophisticated force.[5] The leadership believed this fundamental change was needed to improve China's influence in regional and global affairs, enhance its prestige at home, deter any overt threats to Chinese interests, offset Japan's resurgence, and upgrade its ability to directly use force to protect these aims.[6] However, Deng knew that these ideas were not enough, and that the military leadership also needed to form a strategy to aggressively pursue these objectives. The strategy became the implementation of his four modernizations, both in a generic, mutually supportive sense and in a specific, material manner.

First, modernizing agriculture and making it more productive would permit state support to concentrate on the other three areas. Then, for military needs, since the three modernizations closely complimented each other, and partially overlapped, advances in each could collectively help the others to improve further and faster.

Although the size of China's GNP is very difficult to state authoritatively, it is probably safe to say that with Deng's modernizations it has grown dramatically, with estimates of its doubling or tripling in the past 15 years.[7] The economy accelerated to 8-9 percent annual growth through the 1980s and hit 12.8 percent in 1992.[8] This growth coincided with Deng integrating the defense industry into the national economy. He promoted the concept that as military R&D advances blended into the

4

civilian economy, both would benefit. Building these horizontal links between defense and civilian enterprises would improve communications, enhance production coordination and resource distribution, and help China to compete better in world markets.

Deng also told the military it would have to finance its own modernization. As the GNP of China grew, Deng actually decreased the military's budget in the early 1980s, with the difference going to fund light industry and consumer goods development. He encouraged the military to produce civilian goods using some of its idle production capacity. The result was as desired, with weapon modernization taking place not by prioritizing it without regard to other initiatives (which is how it would have been done in the 1950s and 1960s), but in accordance with a steady improvement in national economic growth.[9] It largely became a "pay as you go" philosophy, something few nations have achieved.

As China's GNP improved, and the military's relationship with civilian industry continued to grow (although they increasingly found themselves in competition with each other), the leadership saw an opportunity to convert its production of low and in some cases middle technology military equipment to its financial advantage.

EXPORT SUCCESS

The PRC's military export program began in earnest in the 1970s, expanded in the 1980s, and by the 1990s was, after the former USSR, the US, France, and possibly the UK, the next largest supplier of arms to Third World nations. China is now considered a "full service" exporter, offering entire air, land, and sea systems rather than the previous tendency towards simple copies of basic Soviet army small arms.[10]

Between 1982 and 1989, China exported $7 billion in arms to Third World nations. Its closest Third World competitor was Brazil which sold $1.4 billion.[11] More importantly, contrary to the pre-1978/Deng period when the PRC exported at little or no actual cost to the receiving nations, it was now being done at substantial profit. The PRC had previously tended to export to relatively poor nations, and based it on ideology. Tanzania, the Congo, Sierra Leone, Sudan, and Zaire were typical customers. It also assisted liberation fronts like the Khmer Rouge, and wrote off the costs in an attempt to lead the non-aligned world, fight "imperialist" states and assist "independent" communist states like North Korea and Albania. The equipment eventually matured to include artillery, tanks, basic patrol boats, and basic fighter/trainer aircraft.[12]

When the PRC changed this outlook to one based on profit, their customers changed. Sub-Saharan clients increasingly shifted to Southeast and Southwest Asia states. At one point, 80 percent of China's

6

sales went to the Middle East, with the Iraq-Iran war proving to be a windfall that accounted for 57 percent of PRC weapon exports during that period. Under Deng, all of its customers, with the exception of Pakistan, Thailand, and possibly Burma, pay full price The others get material at reduced prices. During 1982-1989, sales to all nations, not just Third World ones, totaled $13 billion.[13]

As the level of sales climbed and the customers changed, China also improved the technology of its exports (which probably contributed to the shift in customers). Copies of earlier Soviet designs evolved into modern Chinese upgrades in areas such as fire control systems, main battle tanks, and aircraft engines and avionics. It expanded its naval exports to include submarines to Egypt and is currently negotiating with Thailand.[14]

IMPORT STRATEGY

At the same time China was shifting its export markets, it also expanded the sources it was typically seeking for mid to high technology equipment. China's principal suppliers became the Middle Eastern nations, the former USSR, the UK, the US, and France, in that order. Chinese purchases of US military goods blossomed in the early 1980s after the PRC was designated by the US as a "friendly, non-allied nation." US exports ran from $630 million in 1982 to $1.72 billion in 1988 and centered on engines, electronics, and computers.[15]

Even so, unencumbered by certain market restrictions most other nations were adhering to (China does not insist on "end user" certificates stating which country will ultimately receive and use the equipment), the PRC consistently kept its military trade in the black:

US $ MILLIONS[16]

	1985	1986	1987	1988	1989
Exports	675	1,200	1,800	2,600	2,000
Imports	650	550	625	300	100
Arms Balance	+25	+650	+1,175	+2,300	+1,890

Total: +6,040

This relative prosperity allowed China to invest these profits in the former USSR's "fire sale" of high technology equipment. In 1985, China's Central Military Commission had already directed the military to shift its primary mission from an all-out war with the USSR to responding to regional conflicts. Russian and Ukrainian equipment, available at prices no other country could match, even if they possessed the technology, came at the right time for China. Not only would these purchases allow them immediately to upgrade the sophistication of their military, it would also greatly enhance their mobility and provide the "seed-stock" through reverse engineering for them to compete on future world markets with a new era of weaponry and expand its influence in Asia. Equipment they have bought includes air refueling gear and technology, air force and naval versions of advanced SU-27 and MIG-31 fighters, S-300 (SA-12) surface to air/anti-ballistic missile missiles, IL-76 transports, and possibly in the future, TU22 bombers, T-72M tanks, and even an aircraft carrier.[17] Russia says it will not sell these latter types of platforms; however, in 1991 it sold RD-170 joint Russian-Ukrainian produced space launch vehicles to China. These have greater lift capacity than the Chinese equivalent and can be reverse engineered to enhance its own ICBM programs. Known sales of military equipment from Russia to China in 1992 alone totaled $1.2B.[18]

Just as important is a five year military cooperation agreement signed by China and Russia in November of 1993.[19] It will expand the transfer of technology to China by, for example, using 1,500 Russian technicians to coproduce MIG-31s at a facility in south central China.[20] These acquisitions have gone a long way towards offsetting the PRC military's inability to modernize solely through internal reorganizations of its domestic defense industries. Extensive reorganizations in the 1970s

9

and 1980s did help in more efficiently producing lower technology equipment, but throughout the 1980s China continued to lag far behind the former USSR and the US as well as others in a variety of design and production regimes it had devoted considerable effort to.[21] For example, the PRC built over 750 MIG-21s (current PRC designation is the F-7 Xian) in the 1970s and 1980s, but when they attempted to modernize their fleet, the best they could manage was basically a highly modified two engine version of the original MIG-21 design, which dates back to the 1960s. Relatively few of the new version F-8s have been produced. The agreement with Russia to produce MIG-31s, one of the most advanced interceptors in the world, and purchases of SU-27s, which are roughly comparable to the US F-15, equates to a quantum leap in the PRC's acquisition of, and access to advanced fighter aircraft and related technologies.[22]

Alarmed by these initiatives, the US is trying to limit such agreements and at the same time reenter the Chinese market which it has periodically excluded itself from as "punishment" to the Chinese for their human rights and technology transfer indiscretions. One has to wonder who is punishing whom?

Assistant Secretary of Defense Charles W. Freeman, Jr. was in Beijing in November of 1993 conducting the highest level US-PRC military talks in over three years.[23] The US increasingly finds itself caught between trying to influence China's military relationships with border or regional nations like Pakistan, and getting its own industrial complex back into the extremely lucrative Chinese aviation and space markets, generally considered to be the fastest growing in the world. Fine lines distinguish between what US firms can and cannot sell to China, in part depending on their final application, military or civilian.[24]

PAKISTAN: A SPECIAL CASE

China's continuing special relationship with Pakistan demonstrates a final reason for the technology modernization policies China is following, that of assisting and influencing selected neighbors by supplying them with technology they cannot obtain elsewhere, at any price, with the PRC less interested in making a profit and more interested in influencing a region (a return to its arms export approach of the 1960s). Two examples stand out, nuclear technology, and short range ballistic missiles.

China benefited from a similar policy years before when, in 1957, the USSR and China signed the "New Defense Technical Accord" whereby the Soviets gave China plans for, and an actual prototype of, a proven nuclear weapon and related missile technology. In spite of the Soviets' withdrawing the vast majority of their support in 1960, China successfully detonated a non-weaponized nuclear device in October 1964.[25] They have since built up their stockpile to approximately 450 warheads, with about 300 deployed into a modest triad of land-based missiles, submarine-launched missiles, and bomber-delivered gravity weapons.[26] In the past ten years China has singled out Pakistan with which to share this technology. China also has selectively assisted other nations, for example Algeria, with a 15 megawatt nuclear reactor, and in July of 1993 agreed to build a 300 megawatt reactor for Iran, partly in exchange for MIG-29s Iraq lost to Iran during the Gulf War.[27]

China has also shared technology with Israel (PRC M-series missile designs in return for Patriot ABM technology)[28] and sold Silkworm anti-ship missiles to Iran and Iraq, and Dong Feng CSS-2 intermediate range ballistic missiles (IRBM) to Saudi Arabia in 1987 (the Chinese-use version is believed to carry a 3.3 megaton nuclear warhead).[29] However, this has still followed the "acquire technology and make a profit in the process" strategy.

The Pakistani relationship is something quite different. With a per capita GNP of less than $400, a literacy rate of 26 percent, and 80 percent of its exports agriculturally based, Pakistan still has managed to become a nuclear weapons state.[30] Reacting to India's 1974 test of a non-weaponized device, it initially stole European uranium purification centrifuge designs and established an illicit acquisition network to circumvent export control laws and build a gas centrifuge network at Kahuta. By 1991, they had produced 100-200 kilograms of enriched uranium. The key to building their first weapon came earlier when in the 1980s China simply gave them a proven nuclear weapon design (based on their October 17, 1966 test?) and enough enriched uranium to build two bombs.[31] Pakistan proceeded to fabricate the needed components and test them, and probably had its first weapon ready in 1986. By 1992 the Pakistani foreign minister was admitting publicly that they have nuclear weapon components in unassembled configurations, and in November 1993, Benazir Bhutto stated that "rolling back the nuclear program is not feasible. It will not serve the purpose of nuclear non-proliferation in the region."[32]

China also provided missile support to Pakistan. Although it had been selling Syria its 600 kilometer range M-9 at full market price (something of an insult since Syria had helped finance its development), the PRC handled Pakistan's request for an M-series missile quite differently. Although public sources have not proven that China has sold complete M-11 missiles (which have about half the range of the M-9, but carry a larger warhead,[33] allowing Pakistan to threaten Indian cities like New Delhi, Jaipur, and Ahmadabad), evidence suggests a careful program of Chinese management of a Pakistani M-series acquisition program. China has shipped them M-11 transporter erector launchers and associated hardware, and trained Pakistani missile technicians at Chinese facilities.[34] All of this has occurred with more regard to Chinese influence in the program than Chinese interest in making a profit. This approach is in line with what the PRC refers to as charging "friendship prices" to special clients.

Pakistan says any interest they have in the M-11 is for use with area-denial munitions for attacks against Indian airfields. Even if China withholds actual M-11s from Pakistan, Pakistan is working on its own version, the 300 kilometer range Haft-2.[35] China has helped in this effort as well, assisting with the construction of a propellant factory at Havelian, Pakistan.[36]

All of this occurred in spite of PRC promises they would not export such technology to Pakistan. India (predictably) states that Pakistan now has 60 M-11s and is modifying them to extend their range.[37] In a recent move that will likely inspire Pakistan to work even harder, during February 1994 India tested, for the third time, its Agni medium range, surface-to-surface missile, which has a range of 2,200 kilometers. The Indians say the test was successful. The missile has the range to hit anywhere in Pakistan, and well beyond.[38]

Perhaps even more troubling are reports that Iran is sufficiently impressed with Pakistan's work to recommend they engage in a program of nuclear cooperation, with Iran offering to "underwrite" Pakistan's defense budget ($3.5 billion in 1992). Although Pakistan has thus far declined, it stands as one country's estimate of Pakistan's nuclear sophistication.[39] Iran is already receiving PRC help in developing its own short range ballistic missile, the Tondar-68, which reportedly carries a 700 kilogram warhead.[10]

What does the PRC say about all of this? In a February 1994 discussion at the Academy of Military Science at Beijing, PRC, a senior colonel of the People's Liberation Army told this author that the PRC has three rules governing the export of nuclear technology and materials. He stated they must be used for peaceful purposes, be supervised by the International Atomic Energy Agency, and without PRC consensus, assisted nations could not transfer the technology or materials to yet another country.[41]

In follow-on comments during this same discussion, another PLA senior colonel advised that the PRC exports nuclear technology to assist other countries in their own defense, and that the 30 kilowatt "nuclear power station" they developed in Pakistan is for "development assistance only."[12] He was presumably referring to the PRC designed and supplied reactor currently being built at Chama, Pakistan, on the Indus River.[13]

The senior colonel went on to say the US should not concern itself with PRC arms sales, the US and the former USSR have traditionally been the biggest sellers of arms, China is simply developing its economy to modernize its forces and, therefore, better defend itself, and should not be considered a threat to anyone. Additionally, he stated the PRC does not produce chemical weapons (and in a thinly veiled reference to last year's interception of a Chinese ship suspected of carrying chemical stores to Iran), and is very careful about not exporting materials or technology that could assist another nation in developing them.[14]

Jiang Zemin, General Secretary of the Chinese Communist Party has stated that any transfer they participate in contributes to the receiving nation's legitimate self-defense, does not harm the security of the region, and does not affect the internal affairs of other nations.[45] Obviously, there is room for interpretation in adhering to these guidelines.

The US cut off aid to Pakistan in October 1990 when its nuclear program became obvious, and cut military sales to China in August of 1993 over the M-11 controversy. Yet the Clinton Administration is already offering to waive those sanctions if China promises to withhold future transfers.[46] This follows a chronology of events where the US first approved sales of military technology to China in 1985, suspended cooperation in 1989, then announced in 1992 it would send hardware China had already paid for, but had been put in storage for the last three years, then resumed deliveries in early 1993, only to then announce the two-year embargo in August, and then offer in November to ignore it!

EFFECTS

Such US government behavior is recognized by the Chinese for what it is: an on again, off again approach China can toy with to meet their own interests. China signed the Nuclear Non-proliferation Treaty (NPT) in 1992 and now says it will also adhere to the international Missile Technology Control Regime (MTCR) agreement, originally established by a core of fifteen nations to limit the size and range of missiles that can be exported by a producing nation. Yet the Chinese continue to modernize and test their own nuclear stockpile, conducting their largest test ever in 1992, and a more modest 90 kiloton test in October of 1993, well after other nations had independently stopped testing. They are now developing their own SS-25 style mobile ICBM and are attempting to put multiple warheads on their next generation of ICBMs.[47]

What is the net effect of all of this? First, much of what China is exporting will have little direct impact on any single major power, but certainly contributes to increased instability in certain Middle Eastern and Southeast Asian rivalries. China is clearly concerned about a growing Indian naval presence (India has acquired two aircraft carriers from the UK, an ex-Hermes class and an ex-Hercules class) and India's ability to deliver nuclear weapons via some very capable combat aircraft.[18] It appears China is using Pakistan as a hedge to offset India. This conforms to a broader policy of promoting interdependence among those nations bordering China. By acquiring military technology and either selling or very selectively giving it away, China is trying to create or redistribute a power balance it deems appropriate in the region, all the while helping to finance its own military's modernization, and establish itself as a regional superpower many other nations will feel or desire a special relationship with. It sees an opportunity to use its technological growth and nuclear modernization to increase its influence at a time when the US and former USSR are decreasing their traditional military dominance.[19] At the same time, they do not want to push the US too far, so they are periodically willing to half-step their strategy and sign the NPT and agree to adhere to the MTCR.

As the former USSR continues to decline, China is taking maximum advantage of historical opportunism, shifting from a regional power to a regional superpower at the very time the US slowly, but surely disengages itself from the Philippines, South Korea, and, to a lesser degree, Japan. [50] As it continues to see opportunities to exercise greater influence, China will move to build on emerging relationships with its Asian neighbors, all the while pretending to listen to and cooperate with US desires that it limit weapon proliferation.

REGIONAL REACTIONS

What do China's neighbors think about this? It is probably fair to say that each is evaluating its particular relationship to China with a guarded, "How can we best protect ourselves from the PRC's growing influence, but at the same time not antagonize their leadership?"

For example, the economic superpower of the region, Japan, sees a veritable gold mine in China's economic growth, but cannot help but be concerned about China's military modernization. China possessing a massive land army was one thing; building an increasingly capable power projection force, complete with ICBMs, IRBMs, SLBMs, and air-refuelable fighter-bombers carrying nuclear weapons is quite another. Japan is contributing to a multinational fund that will (if it functions properly) track the disposition of Soviet-trained nuclear weapons engineers. Japan may well work with the US in a joint venture similar to the proposed US, and US-Israeli program to produce a regionally deployed anti-ballistic missile defense system. They know that the days of a US nuclear umbrella protecting them from China and the former USSR are probably drawing to some sort of dramatic change or end, especially as the US continues to remove its tactical nuclear weapons from forward deployed locations.[51] Japan is taking some steps to broaden its direct military responsibilities, for example extending its maritime operating area out to 1,000 miles from the home islands. They have also consistently spent considerable funds on maintaining a relatively high technology military force, although in terms of GNP percentages, it is relatively modest.[52] They are willing to pay more and more of the costs of keeping a significant US presence in Japan, but also know that the US alone cannot do it all. They know that in the long run they must accept China's growing influence as a reality and work with them rather than try to follow a policy of aloofness or isolation.

The next largest economic powers, South Korea and Taiwan, considering their relative economic strength compared to Japan, have taken a militarily more proactive stance, consistently spending large sums buying US combat aircraft and building capable naval combat surface fleets. Both have done preliminary work on nuclear weapons programs, and probably would have moved further along in them if the US had not pressured them into restraint. South Korea, of course, maintains a large standing army, obviously to keep the North at bay. Taiwan uses its 100-mile wide Formosa Strait to serve as a substitute for such an army, and is quietly, but nervously watching the PRC grow militarily and economically. As a result, Taiwan periodically buys arms from the US (for example, F-16s) to strengthen its position, much to the annoyance of the PRC.

A pattern emerges as we move away from the developed, and newly industrialized nations and look at resource-rich developing nations such as Indonesia, Malaysia, Thailand, and the Philippines. Although not as prosperous as Japan, South Korea, or Taiwan, they still spend what they think they can afford (or in the case of the Philippines, more than they can afford) to maintain a viable military posture. These nations in the past had placed their emphasis on counterinsurgency forces to handle their internal problems, but are now investing in limited power projection navies and air forces, just like China. All are quietly and carefully reexamining their relationships and options with the US and with Australia, cooperating with them in ways (joint exercises, and port and airfield transit access) they were not comfortable with 5-15 years ago.[53]

India, like Pakistan, is something of a special case, but not because it has warmed up to China, but for just the opposite reason. With the demise of the Soviet Union, India lost its most powerful ally and primary supplier of arms. It needs the US to help it with the multi-billion dollar loans it gets from the International Monetary Fund. Plus, India has had a history of border clashes with China. Consequently, although New Delhi may periodically look like it is thawing its relationship with Beijing, it probably is not, especially as long as China continues to aid Pakistan. In an effort to offset China's interest in power projection, India has gone so far as to recommend joint US-Indian sea lane patrols.[54]

Paradoxically, as all of these nations take steps to offset China's growing influence, its fellow communist states may be the ones who suffer most from future Chinese direct military force. Vietnam was invaded by China not long after the US-Vietnam War, and could fight again over oil and the Spratly Islands. China's solidarity with North Korea has slipped over the years, and small nations like Laos remember China's history of overwhelming border regions when it suits its purpose.

One move that probably benefits most of China's neighbors was a late 1992-early 1993 "velvet purge" of the Chinese military leadership by the 89-year-old Deng. A year ago he quietly began to shift senior officers into retirement or less influential positions when he suspected they were working on a post-Deng succession plan.[55] Hopefully, this will moderate any inclination by the military to use its strength to settle future, near-term differences with its neighbors.

CONCLUSION

In summary, China's military restructuring and modernization has to make its neighbors nervous. Shifting from a lumbering giant to a modern, mobile force gives it a high technology power projection capability it has never had before. As Australian analyst Gary Klintworth writes, countries like Thailand and Vietnam "have come to terms with the fact that China will become the dominant great power in Asia."[56] This is at least in part due to what they are doing with their military and defense industry reorganization and modernization. China's neighbors, and the US, are grudgingly accepting the idea that in most cases they need to adjust their relationships accordingly.

Historically, China's turn to be the dominant force in Asia may have arrived. As Nicholas Kristof states, "China is not a villain. It is not a renegade country, but rather an ambitious nation."[57] He explains what many Americans do not want to hear, namely, that the country we came to view with such trepidation in the first 40 years of its existence has in many respects come of age, complete with the fastest growing economy in the world and possibly the fastest growing military budget--at the very time virtually every other nation in the world is cutting back their defense budgets.[58]

Who would have imagined a few years ago that the PRC would work out an arrangement, as they apparently have done, with Burma to develop two islands in the Indian Ocean (no part of China even comes close to touching the Indian Ocean) as observation posts. Will, as Kristof suggests, these eventually grow into a naval base for the PRC?[59] One can laugh at the suggestion, but is the idea so different from the UK base at Diego Garcia the US Navy and Air Force have grown accustomed to using?

Kristof cautions us that the international community is fond of expressing wonderment at the extraordinary changes taking place in China, but is failing to appreciate "the colossal implications of the rise of a powerful China."[60]

He is right. They are not a villain. They have as much right to modernize and improve on the efficiency of their military as we do. But that does not mean we should not watch their progress carefully, or stumble over ourselves in continuing to shift our approach to dealing with China with all of the subtlety of a sailor on 24-hour shore leave. The United States needs to determine what China's mid-range objectives are as they convert to a force structure increasingly capable of exerting influence beyond their borders. We need to prepare ourselves and our allies accordingly. As Admiral Charles R. Larson, USN, Commander in Chief, US Pacific Command, stated to the Senate Armed Services

Committee in April, 1993, "China places high premium on better relations with the US but is prepared for a long period of increased tensions. . . . In the final analysis, I believe the best approach to dealing with China's continuing growth in both economic and military arenas is to engage Beijing in a dialogue aimed at fostering cooperation and avoiding the development of a peer competitor in Asia.[61]

Sound advice. The challenge will be in establishing a dialogue that will allow both the US and the PRC to achieve their respective goals in Asia.

NOTES

1. Thomas Baranauskas and Thalif Deen, "China (PRC)," *Forecast International/DMS Market Intelligence Report (Jane's)*, (Newtown, CN: Jane's Information Group, July 1993), pg. 5.

2. Mark Wah Lee, "The Chinese Defense Industrial Reforms: Hindering or Promoting Military Modernization?" Masters Thesis, University of Texas at Austin (August 1990), pg. 8-11.

3. Ibid.

4. Frederic M. Kaplan, *Encyclopedia of China Today* (New York: Harper and Row, 1979), pg. 225.

5. Susan V. Lawrence, "Still on the March," *U.S. News and World Report*, 9 March 1992, pg. 36-9.

6. Bonnie S. Glaser, "China's Security Perceptions," *Asian Survey*, vol. xxxiii, no. 3: 721 (March 1993).

7. Mortimer B. Zuckerman, "China's New Reality," *U.S. News and World Report*, 15 March 1993, pg. 76.

8. Baranauskas and Deen, pg. 11.

9. Lee, pg. 12.

10. Richard A. Bitzinger, "Chinese Arms Production and Sales To The Third World," *RAND Note N-3334-USDP*, (Santa Monica, 1992), pg. 1.

11. Bitzinger, pg. 3-12.

12. Ibid.

13. Ibid.

14. Ibid.

15. Baranauskas and Deen, pg. 11-13.

16. Anon., "U. S. Trade With China," U. S. Department of State *Dispatch*, 24 June 1991, pg. 456.

17. Michael T. Klare, "The Next Great Arms Race," *Foreign Affairs*, Summer 1993, vol. 72, no. 3: pg. 141-143. Also see Michael Mecham, "China Updates Its Military, But Business Comes First," *Aviation Week and Space Technology*, 15 March 1993, pg. 58.

18. Theresa Foley, " Bush, Clinton Blink At Secret Purchase of Zenit Engines," *Space News*, 1-7 November 1993, pg. 1.

19. Patrick E. Tyler, "Russia and China Sign A Military Agreement," *New York Times*, 10 November 1993, pg. 15.

20. David A. Fulghum, "China Seeks To Build MIG-31," *Aviation Week and Space Technology*, 5 October 1992, pg. 27.

21. Paul H. B. Godwin, *The Chinese Communist Armed Forces* (Maxwell Air Force Base, AL: Air University Press, 1988), pg. 75.

22. Derek Wood, *Jane's World Aircraft Recognition Handbook* (Coulsdon, UK: Jane's Information Group, 1989), pg. 105, 107, 202.

23. Lena Sun, "U.S. Military Talks in Beijing Productive," *Washington Post*, 3 November 1993, pg. 12.

24. R. Jeffery Smith, "U. S. Offers to Waive Chine Trade Sanctions," *Washington Post*, 11 November 1993, pg. 39.

25. Richard Fieldhouse, "China's Mixed Signals On Nuclear Weapons," *The Bulletin of the Atomic Scientists*, May 1991, pg. 40. It is interesting to note that 47 Chinese nuclear scientists continued to quietly do research in the Soviet Union until June, 1965. See Larry M. Wortzel, *China's Military Modernization* (Westport, CN: Greenwood Press, Inc., 1988), pg. 30.

26. Anon., "Chinese Nuclear Forces," *The Bulletin of the Atomic Scientists*, November 1993, pg. 57.

27. John M. Deutsch, "The New Nuclear Threat," *Foreign Affairs*, vol. 71, no. 4: 131 (Fall 1992).

28. David A. Fulghum, "Defense Department Confirms Patriot Technology Diverted," *Aviation Week and Space Technology*, 1 February 1993, pg. 26.

29. Fieldhouse, pg. 41.

30. Pervez Hoodbhoy, "Myth-building: The 'Islamic' Bomb," *The Bulletin of the Atomic Scientists*, June 1993, pg. 47-8.

31. David Albright, "A Proliferation Primer," *The Bulletin of the Atomic Scientists*, June 1993, pg. 16-22.

32. Anon., "Pakistan Will Not Abandon Nuclear Plan," *Baltimore Sun*, 21 November 1993, pg. 11. Also see Emily MacFarguhar, "Breaking A Chain Reaction," *U. S. News and World Report*, 9 March 1992, pg. 43.

33. Jaime A. Florcurz. "For Sale: Tools of Destruction," *Time*, 22 April 1991, pg. 44.

34. Smith, pg. 39. Also see Lawrence E. Grinter, "The United States and South Asia: New Challenges, New Opportunities," *Asian Affairs*, Summer 1993, pg. 104.

35. Simon Henderson, "We Can Do It Ourselves," *The Bulletin of the Atomic Scientists*, September 1993, pg. 29.

36. R. R. Subramanian, *India, Pakistan, China* (New Delhi, India: ABC Publishing House, 1989), pg. 82-83.

37. Folghum, pg. 27.

38. Smith, pg. 39.

39. Mitchell Reiss, "Safeguarding The Nuclear Peace in South Asia," *Asian Survey*, vol. xxxiii, no. 12, December 1993, pg. 1112.

40. Roy Braybrook, "Ballistic Missiles a Growing Threat," *Asia-Pacific Defence Reporter*, October-November 1993, pg. 32.

41. Meeting, U. S. Air Force Air War College Delegation and Members of the People's Republic of China People's Liberation Army Academy of Military Science, Beijing, PRC, February 16, 1994.

42. Ibid.

43. Henderson, pg. 30.

44. Meeting, U. S. Air Force Air War College Delegation and PRC PLA Academy of Military Science.

45. Mortimer Zuckerman, "China's Arms Sales Are Very Limited," *U. S. News and World Report*, 15 March 1993, pg. 60.

46. Smith, pg. 39.

47. Jim Mann, "China Upgrading Nuclear Arms, Experts Say, " *Los Angeles Times*, Washington Edition, 9 November 1993, pg. 20.

48. Bernard Prezelin, *Combat Fleets of the World*, 1993 (Annapolis MD: Naval Institute Press) 1993, pg. 250.

49. Glaser, pg. 267-9.

50. Baranauskas and Deen, pg. 10.

51. Ryukichi Imai, "Asian Ambitions, Rising Tensions" *The Bulletin of the Atomic Scientists*, June 1993, pg. 35-6.

52. Klare, pg. 143-144.

53. Pete Engario, "Beijing Is On An Arms Binge, And The Neighbors Are Nervous," *Business Week*, 6 July 1992, pg. 49.

54. MacFarguar, pg. 43.

55. Joyce Barnathan, "Does Deng's Army Shakeup Mean Reform Is A Surer Thing?" *Business Week*, 1 February 1993, pg. 43.

56. Engario, pg. 49.

57. Nicholas D. Kristof, "The Rise of China," *Foreign Affairs*, November-December 1993, vol. 72, no. 5, pg. 73.

58. Ibid., pg. 59.

59. Ibid., pg. 67.

60. Ibid., pg. 60-61.

61. Admiral Charles R. Larson, USN. "United States Pacific Command Posture Statement," (unpublished) May 1993, pg. 12-14.

BIBLIOGRAPHY

1. Albright, David. "A Proliferation Primer," *The Bulletin of the Atomic Scientists*, June 1993.

2. *Baltimore Sun*, 21 November 1993.

3. Baranauskas, Tom and Deen, Thalif. "China (PRC) Data," *Forecast International/DMS Market Survey/Intelligence Report (Jane's)*, July 1993.

4. Barnathan, Joyce. "Does Deng's Army Shakeup Mean Reform Is A Surer Thing?" *Business Week*, 1 February 1993.

5. Bitzinger, Richard A. "Chinese Arms Production and Sales To The Third World," *RAND Note N-3334-USDP*, 1992.

6. Braybrook, Roy. "Ballistic Missiles A Growing Threat," *Asia-Pacific Defence Reporter* Octob.r-.Jovember 1993.

7. Deutsch, John M. "The New Nuclear Threat," *Foreign Affairs*, vol. 71, no. 4, Fall 1992.

8. Engario, Pete. "Beijing Is On An Arms Binge, And The Neighbors Are Nervous" *Business Week*, 6 July 1992.

9. Fieldhouse, Richard. "China's Mixed Signals On Nuclear Weapons," *The Bulletin of the Atomic Scientists*, May 1991.

10. Florcruz, Jaime A. "For Sale: Tools Of Destruction," *Time*, 22 April 1991.

11. Foley, Theresa. "Bush, Clinton Blink At Secret Purchase of Zenit Engines," *Space News*, 1-7 November, 1993.

12. Fulghum, David A. "China Seeks To Build MIG-31," *Aviation Week and Space Technology*, 5 October 1992.

13. Fulghum, David A. "Defense Department Confirms Patriot Technology Diverted," *Aviation Week and Space Technology*, 1 February 1993.

14. Glazer, Bonnie S. "China's Security Perceptions," *Asian Survey*, vol. xxxiii, no. 3, March 1993.

15. Godwin, Paul H. B. *The Chinese Communist Armed Forces*, (Maxwell Air Force Base, AL, Air University Press), 1988..

16. Grinter, Lawrence E., "The United States and South Asia: New Challenges, New Opportunities," *Asian Affairs*, Summer, 1993.

17. Henderson, Simon. "We Can Do It Ourselves," *The Bulletin of the Atomic Scientists*, September 1993.

18. Hoodbhoy, Pervez. "Myth-building: The 'Islamic' Bomb," *The Bulletin of the Atomic Scientists*, June 1993.

19. Imai, Ryukichi. "Asian Ambitions, Rising Tensions," *The Bulletin of the Atomic Scientists*, June 1993.

20. Kaplan, Frederic M. *Encyclopedia of China Today*, (New York, Harper and Row), 1979.

21. Klare, Michael T. "The Next Great Arms Race," *Foreign Affairs*, vol. 72, no. 3, Summer 1993.

22. Kristof, Nicholas D. "The Rise of China," *Foreign Affairs*, November-December 1993.

23. Larson, Charles R. Admiral, USN. "United States Pacific Command Posture Statement." (unpublished) May 1993.

24. Lawrence, Susan V. "Still On The March," *U. S. News and World Report*, 9 March 1992.

25. Lee, Mark Wah. "The Chinese Defense Industrial Reforms: Hindering Or Promoting Military Modernization?," Master's thesis, University of Texas at Austin, 1990.

26. MacFarquhar, Emily. "Breaking A Chain Reaction," *U.S. News and World Report*, 9 March 1992.

27. Mann, Jim. "China Upgrading Nuclear Arms, Experts Say," *Los Angeles Times*, Washington Edition, 9 November 1993.

28. Mecham, Michael. "China Updates Its Military, But Business Comes First," *Aviation Week and Space Technology*, 15 March 1993.

29. *Montgomery Advertiser.* "India Tests Ballistic Missile," 20 February 1994.

30. Prezelin, Bernard. *Combat Fleets of the World,* (Annapolis MD, Naval Institute Press), 1993.

31. Reiss, Mitchell. "Safeguarding The Nuclear Peace in South Asia," *Asian Survey,* vol. xxxiii, no. 12, Dec 1993.

32. Smith, R. Jeffery. "U. S. Offers To Waive China Trade Sanctions," *Washington Post,* 11 November 1993.

33. Subramanion, R. R. *India, Pakistan, China,* (New Delhi, India, ABC Publishing House), 1989.

34. Sun, Lena. "U. S. Military Talks In Beijing Productive," *Washington Post,* 3 November 1993.

35. *The Bulletin of the Atomic Scientists,* "Chinese Nuclear Forces," November 1993.

36. Tyler, Patrick E. "Russia and China Sign A Military Agreement," *New York Times,* 10 November 1993.

37. U. S. Department of State *Dispatch,* "U. S. Trade With China," 24 June 1991.

38. Wood, Derek. *Jane's World Aircraft Recognition Handbook,* (Coulsdon, U.K., Jane's Information Group), 1989.

39. Zuckerman, Mortimer B. "China's New Reality," *U. S. News and World Report,* 15 March 1993.